D0734740

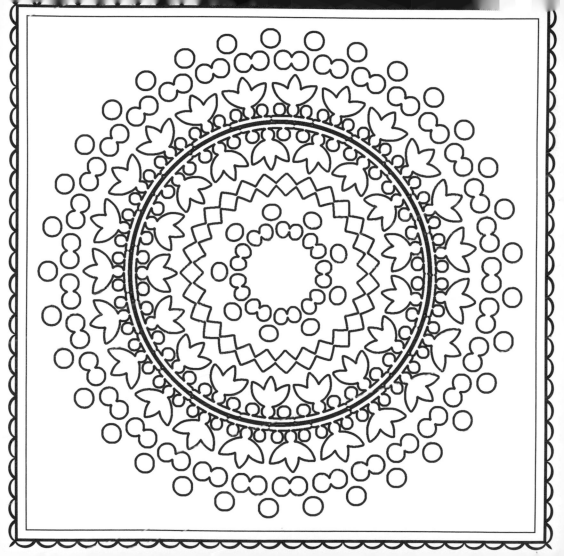

Look for these other titles in the Mini Pads of Color series by Barron's

DREAMS OF FLOWERS — ISBN 978-1-4380-1009-0

SEA OF FLOWERS — ISBN 978-1-4380-1012-0

MANDALA DELIGHTS — ISBN 978-1-4380-1010-6

All inquiries should be addressed to:
Barron's Educational Series, Inc.
250 Wireless Boulevard
Hauppauge, New York 11788
www.barronseduc.com

ISBN: 978-1-4380-1011-3
Illustrations: Getty Images / Thinkstock; Fotolia: buja_gatta, Irina Markovskaya, katyau, transistock
Printed in China
9 8 7 6 5 4 3 2 1

First English-language edition published in 2017 by
Barron's Educational Series, Inc.
Original German title: Mandalazauber
© Copyright 2016 arsEdition GmbH, München

All rights reserved.
No part of this book may be reproduced in any form or by any means without the written permission of the copyright owner.